Nadeem Lutfullah

DEATH OF THE RÉSUMÉ. WHAT'S NEXT?

A bold manifesto for those ready to outpace algorithms, redefine relevance and take back control, in a world where visibility, adaptability and skill are the new currency of success.

Self-published.
Dubai, United Arab Emirates.

Copyright © 2025 Nadeem Shafkat Lutfullah

Nadeem Shafkat Lutfullah asserts the moral right to be identified as the author of this work. All rights reserved. No part of this publication may be reproduced, stored in a retrieval system, or transmitted in any form or by any means – electronic, mechanical, photocopying, recording or otherwise – without prior written permission from the author.

Unauthorized actions relating to this publication may result in civil liability and damages.

Title: *Death of the Résumé*
Print Edition ISBN: 978-969-8392-58-1
First Edition: 2025
Cover Design by: Arsalan Ali
Published by: Self-published
Edited and Typeset by: Matt McAvoy
Author's Website: www.thecareerceo.com
LinkedIn Profile: www.linkedin.com/in/nadeem-lutfullah
YouTube Channel: www.youtube.com/@nadeemlutfullah

For information on bulk purchases, please visit Amazon.com.

Acknowledgments

I wish to acknowledge the inspiration, insight and generous support of several professionals who have shaped my thinking and practice in this ever-evolving space of mentoring, leadership, careers and recruitment.

This book is dedicated to the following individuals – selfless leaders, mentors, fellow career architects, ex-colleagues and trailblazers – whose work and connection have profoundly enriched my journey. Your presence, contributions over the past several years and commitment to excellence have helped shape the ideas within these pages, and strengthened my resolve to keep giving back. Thank you.

With deep appreciation:

Anna Power

Betania Allo

Damian Ellacott

David Alto

Derick Mildred

Dr. Dorothy Kyeyune

Dr. Jonathan R. Tuck

Dr. Khurram Nawaz

Fabien Ghys

Faran Niaz

Grace Karim

Hugh Maxwell

John Espirian

Joseph Gonzalez

Mohammed Sadek

Saleem Golandaz

Salman Sarwar

Samir Barot

Scott Derbyshire

Somia Anwar

Taher Alkhaja

Talha Shaikh

Ufaq Ali

A Quick Note Before You Begin

If you find value in the insights shared in this book, I'd be truly grateful if you could leave a brief, honest review on the platform where you purchased it.

Your feedback not only helps others discover the book; it also plays a small but meaningful part in shaping better career journeys for others.

Thank you.

Table of Contents

Preface 1

1. The Rise and Fall 9
    The Origins of Professional Documentation 9
    The Technological Shift: From Paper to Digital 14
    Conclusion 15
    Digital Revolution in Hiring 16
    The Rise of Applicant Tracking Systems (ATS) 18
    LinkedIn's Disruption of Traditional Résumés 19
    The ATS Paradox: Efficiency vs. Exclusion 21
    The Beginning of the End for the Résumé? 23

2. The AI Revolution Begins 24
    AI's Disruption of Traditional Recruitment 24
    Predictive Hiring: A Next-Gen Shift in Talent
    Selection 25
    Skills Over Credentials: The New Hiring Standard
    30
    Automated Candidate Discovery: The Shift from
    Reactive to Proactive Hiring 33

3. New Ways to Shine 37
    Asynchronous Video Interviews 37
    Lights, Camera, You're Hired! 44
    The Future of Digital Professional Profiles 46
    Hiring Through Play: Gamified Recruitment 55
    AI-Driven Skill-Assessment Platforms 62

4. Mastering the Future 68
    Building Your AI-Proof Digital Presence 68
    Self-Audit 78
    Skills of the Future Workforce; The Three
    Interconnected Pillars 83
    Building a Personalized Skill-Development Plan . 88
    Demonstrating Future-Ready Skills 89
    Personal Branding Strategy 90
    Five Transition Success Stories 93

About the Author 105

Also by Nadeem Lutfullah 106

Preface

The résumé is dying.

For years, I had sensed an undercurrent of transformation in the hiring world—subtle at first, but steadily gaining momentum. As someone deeply entrenched in recruitment and career strategy, I observed how technology, shifting work-life dynamics in a post-pandemic world and, most recently, artificial intelligence, were converging to rewrite the rules of employment. What had once been a structured, predictable process was now evolving into something entirely different, something that rendered the traditional résumé increasingly obsolete.

And so, here I am, writing about the very document that has shaped careers for generations, yet now stands on the brink of irrelevance. After decades of studying, refining and guiding countless professionals through the art of résumé-building, I find myself advocating for its impending demise.

The word "regret" does not exist in my dictionary; therefore, I feel only a sense of relief and responsibility.

Relief because I have moved beyond the internal resistance and uncertainty that once accompanied my realization of the résumé's diminishing relevance. Accepting this inevitable shift was not immediate; it required breaking free from long-held conventions and acknowledging the transformation already unfolding in the hiring world. And responsibility because, having gained this clarity, I now feel compelled to help others recognize and prepare for what lies ahead. The future of hiring will not wait for those reluctant to adapt. Staying informed is the first step, and proactive preparation is the key to surviving and thriving in this new era.

A quiet revolution is unfolding in the hiring industry: innovative organizations abandoning résumés in favor of methods that better predict performance and potential. These companies are not just changing their hiring processes; they are gaining competitive advantages by finding talent others missed.

This book is not about speculation; it is a guide to readiness and empowerment. While no one can predict with absolute certainty how quickly or extensively these changes will unfold, the trajectory is undeniable. The strategies and insights shared here will equip professionals to stay ahead of the curve, ensuring that, when these shifts take full effect, they will be prepared to navigate challenges with confidence, seize emerging opportunities and secure lasting success.

For decades, the résumé has been the unquestioned gatekeeper of professional opportunity. This single document has determined who gets interviews, who advances careers and who gets left behind. We've accepted this system despite its obvious flaws: its inability to capture soft skills, its bias toward certain backgrounds and its reduction of complex human potential to bullet points. But now, powerful forces are rendering the traditional résumé obsolete.

Artificial intelligence, skills-based hiring platforms and digital portfolios are rapidly transforming how companies identify and evaluate talent. Major organizations like Tesla, IBM and Google have already moved away from résumé-centric hiring, recognizing that the traditional approach fails to identify the best candidates in today's complex job market. The shift isn't just coming, it's already here.

You might be wondering why this matters to you.

Whether you're someone looking for a job who is frustrated by sending résumés into the void, a hiring manager drowning in applications or a professional trying to advance your career, the death of the résumé will fundamentally change how you work, how you find work and how you progress in your career. The rules that governed professional advancement for generations are being rewritten.

The question isn't whether the résumé will fade away, it's whether you'll be prepared when it does.

The death of the résumé isn't happening in isolation; it's part of a broader transformation in how we think about work, careers and professional identity. The linear career paths of previous generations have given way to more fluid professional journeys. The skills that matter most are changing faster than traditional credentials can keep pace with. And technology is creating new possibilities for demonstrating capabilities that weren't previously available.

In the first chapter, we will trace the evolution of the résumé, from its origins to its current limitations. You will learn how what began as a useful tool became an increasingly problematic barrier between talent and opportunity. We will examine how LinkedIn and the Applicant Tracking Systems (ATS) attempted to modernize the résumé, but ultimately reinforced many of its fundamental flaws.

Chapter 2 explores the AI revolution transforming hiring practices. You'll discover how predictive algorithms, skills-based assessments and intelligent discovery platforms are creating more accurate ways to match people with opportunities. We'll look at real examples of companies abandoning résumés in favor of these approaches, and the results they're achieving.

In Chapter 3, we will examine the new tools and platforms emerging to replace the traditional résumé. From asynchronous video interviews to gamified assessments, and digital portfolios to reputation systems, you will learn about the diverse alternatives providing richer pictures of professional capabilities. This chapter includes practical guidance on using these tools effectively.

Finally, Chapter 4 provides a comprehensive roadmap for thriving in the post-résumé world. You will learn specific strategies for developing an AI-proof professional identity, and crafting a personal brand that resonates with both human reviewers and machine-based evaluators. The chapter also includes success stories from professionals who have already made this transition. These individuals succeeded by embracing the very strategies, tools and mindset shifts outlined in this book.

Throughout this book, you will find that I take a balanced approach. While I believe the traditional résumé is dying, I recognize that the transition won't happen overnight, or uniformly across all industries. Some sectors will change faster than others, and hybrid approaches will emerge during the transition. My goal is to prepare you for what's coming, not to suggest that résumés will completely disappear tomorrow.

You will also notice that I focus on practical application rather than theoretical possibilities. The strategies and approaches I share in this book have been tested in real-world settings, with real people navigating career transitions. This isn't about futuristic speculation, it's about concrete steps you can take today to position yourself for success as hiring practices evolve.

The "death of the résumé" represents both challenge and

opportunity. For job-seekers, it means learning new ways to showcase talents and connect with opportunities. For recruiters and hiring managers, it offers the possibility of finding better matches and building stronger teams. For everyone, it requires rethinking how we present our professional selves in a rapidly changing corporate environment.

The good news is that the alternatives emerging to replace the résumé often provide more authentic, multi-dimensional and exciting ways to demonstrate capabilities. Rather than reducing complex human potential to standardized formats, these new approaches allow for more personalized expression of skills and attributes. They create space for qualities that traditional résumés fail to capture: creativity, adaptability, emotional intelligence and unique perspectives.

As we explore this transformation together, I invite you to approach the journey with both openness and healthy skepticism. Question assumptions about how hiring should work. Experiment with new ways of presenting your professional self. And remember that behind all the technology and trends are human beings, seeking meaningful connections through work.

The résumé as we've known it is dying. What comes next will be more dynamic, more personalized and potentially more equitable. This book is your guide to navigating that future, whether you're looking to advance your own career or to hire new talent. The transformation is already visible on the hiring horizon.

Adapt or fade.

1.
The Rise and Fall

The Origins of Professional Documentation

The practice of documenting one's professional qualifications has evolved over centuries. While ancient Egyptian craftsmen carved intricate designs and hieroglyphs into stone tablets, these works primarily served religious, funerary or commemorative purposes. The concept of a structured document showcasing an individual's professional skills and accomplishments, akin to the modern résumé, would take much longer to emerge.

Notably, in 1482, Leonardo da Vinci penned a letter to Ludovico Sforza, the future Duke of Milan, detailing his capabilities, a document often regarded as one of the earliest résumés. These early forms of professional documentation weren't merely practical tools; they represented something deeper about human nature: our fundamental need to be recognized for our skills and contributions.

The Renaissance and Age of Exploration brought new

forms of professional documentation. As European powers established colonial outposts and trading companies, they needed ways to evaluate workers for positions abroad. The Dutch East India Company, founded in 1602, developed one of the first standardized application processes, requiring candidates to submit written accounts of their previous voyages, skills and references from ship captains. These documents, stored in company archives, allowed administrators to make hiring decisions for positions remotely, a challenge that still resonates in today's globally connected job market.

Centuries later, the Industrial Revolution marked a turning point in the history of professional documentation. As businesses moved from small workshops to large factories, the personal connections that had governed employment for centuries began to break down. Factory owners needed efficient ways to evaluate large numbers of potential workers, while the candidates needed ways to market themselves to employers they might never meet face-to-face.

This period saw the emergence of the "letter of introduction", a forerunner to the modern résumé. These letters typically combined personal information, work history and character references in a single document. Employers often seemed to prioritize the workers' moral character and reliability, sometimes considering technical skills as secondary. This emphasis reflected their concerns about maintaining discipline and integrity within burgeoning industries.

The late nineteenth century brought another shift, as industrialization matured and specialized roles proliferated. Companies began requesting more specific information about candidates' skills and experience. Employment agencies emerged as intermediaries, creating early standardized forms to collect consistent information from job-seekers. Toward the end of the century, employment agencies increasingly sought comprehensive information from candidates, including their employment history and reasons for leaving previous positions – categories that remain standard on résumés until today.

The modern résumé, as we know it, began to take shape in the early twentieth century. The growing complexity of business organizations created demand for specialized roles, while advances in transportation made workforce mobility more common. Workers needed portable documents that could quickly communicate their qualifications to potential employers in different cities, and spread across different industries.

World War One accelerated this trend, as governments mobilized millions of civilians for military and industrial roles. The U.S. military developed standardized personnel forms to track soldiers' civilian skills and assign them appropriately – systems that many veterans continued to use when seeking employment after the war. These forms emphasized efficiency and standardization, reducing complex work histories to simple chronological listings.

Next, the post-World War Two economic boom cemented the résumé's central role in hiring. As corporations expanded and professional management techniques spread, human resources departments sought systematic approaches to evaluating candidates. This led to the emergence of the chronological résumé format, which listed education and work experience in reverse order, to prioritize recent accomplishments.

By the 1950s, career counselors and employment agencies had codified résumé-writing conventions that would remain largely unchanged for decades: one or two pages, chronological format, emphasis on credentials and work history, and minimal personal information. These conventions reflected the needs of large corporate employers, processing high volumes of applications through increasingly bureaucratic hiring systems. During this era, lifetime employment was the norm. Once hired, employees relied on internal promotions rather than job-hopping, so résumés were primarily used for internal career transitions.

However, the limitations of this standardization soon became apparent. The chronological résumé worked well for traditional career paths, but disadvantaged those with employment gaps, career shifts or unconventional experience. It emphasized credentials over actual abilities, failing to capture critical soft skills like leadership, adaptability and creativity.

By the 1960s, concerns about these limitations surfaced. A 1962 *Personnel Journal* article highlighted that résumés were often *"misleading and incomplete"*, failing to reflect essential qualities, such as problem-solving ability and interpersonal strengths. Despite these concerns, the efficiency of standardized résumés ensured their continued dominance in hiring.

The Technological Shift: From Paper to Digital

Technological advances in the late twentieth century transformed the résumé's format, but not its fundamental structure. The advent of word processors made it easier to create, edit and tailor résumés for specific job applications. Fax machines and email further revolutionized résumé distribution, allowing candidates to submit applications instantly, instead of mailing printed copies.

The 1990s introduced the first online job boards, dramatically changing the job application process. Platforms like The Monster Board (1994) enabled employers to post job openings online and receive applications from a global talent pool. This expanded access to opportunities beyond local markets, reshaping recruitment strategies.

However, these digital platforms also created a résumé flood; companies suddenly received thousands of applications per position. This volume overwhelmed hiring teams, leading to the rise of *applicant tracking systems*

(ATS) in the late 1990s. ATS software scanned résumés for specific keywords and predefined criteria, filtering out those that didn't match the system's programmed requirements. This reinforced résumé standardization, as job-seekers began optimizing résumés for ATS readability rather than human review.

While ATS improved efficiency, it also introduced biases that disadvantaged highly capable candidates who lacked exact keyword matches.

Despite these changes, the fundamental issues with résumés persisted. The reliance on past experience and credentials remained, even though hiring managers increasingly recognized that these factors alone did not predict job performance.

As workforce diversity increased and career paths became less linear, the résumé's flaws became more pronounced, setting the stage for new hiring innovations that would challenge its dominance.

Conclusion

Understanding this historical context is crucial, as it provides valuable insight into how hiring practices evolved, shedding light on past limitations, and equipping them with the knowledge to steer through and adapt to the future of recruitment with confidence.

Résumés have been essential in the hiring process for over a century, adapting to changes in industry, technology and workforce expectations. However, their persistence, despite well-documented limitations, suggests they are more than just documents; they are institutions deeply embedded in hiring practices.

The résumé's role as a gatekeeper to employment opportunities has remained, even as technology and talent-focused hiring challenge its relevance. As we move into an era shaped by machine-led recruitment, digital portfolios and real-time skill assessments, the question remains: is the résumé ultimately becoming obsolete?

Digital Revolution in Hiring

The digital revolution of the 1990s transformed virtually every aspect of business, but few areas changed as dramatically as hiring. The résumé, which had remained largely unchanged for decades, suddenly found itself at the center of a technological shift. The widespread adoption of the internet led to the emergence of online job boards, fundamentally altering how employers and job-seekers connected.

The earliest digital résumés emerged in the late 1980s and early 1990s, as simple word processor documents. Job-seekers with personal computers – still a relative luxury – gained a distinct advantage in producing clean, error-free documents that could be updated easily. Microsoft Word, which launched in 1983 and became widely adopted in the early 1990s, introduced résumé templates that further standardized formats.

By 1993, email was becoming common in corporate environments, allowing for rapid résumé submissions. However, the true transformation came with the launch of the first online job boards. The Online Career Center (OCC), founded in 1992, and The Monster Board (1994), revolutionized how job-seekers found opportunities and how employers sourced candidates. Unlike newspaper classifieds, online job boards allowed companies to post detailed job descriptions and access talent pools beyond local markets.

By 1998, specialized job boards targeting specific

industries emerged, refining digital résumés even further. Each industry developed its own formatting conventions, aligning résumés with sector-specific hiring standards.

The Rise of Applicant Tracking Systems (ATS)

By the early 2000s, the explosion of online applications created a new challenge: recruiters were overwhelmed by the sheer volume of submissions. This led to the widespread adoption of applicant tracking systems (ATS), which enabled employers to manage digital résumés more efficiently. ATS, initially introduced in the 1990s, became an industry standard in the 2000s, helping companies filter and rank applications based on keyword searches and predefined criteria.

Taleo, one of the earliest major ATS platforms, processed applications for over three hundred corporations by 2003, fundamentally altering résumé evaluation. This shift introduced new barriers: while job boards had democratized access to opportunities, ATS narrowed the selection process through machine-based filtering mechanisms. The ideal candidate could now be excluded from consideration simply because their résumé lacked the right keywords or formatting. Résumé writing became increasingly technical, requiring job-seekers to optimize their documents for automation-based filtering systems rather than human readers.

Despite its flaws, ATS adoption surged throughout the 2000s, becoming a standard tool for handling high application volumes. By automating résumé screening, these systems reshaped hiring workflows but also introduced new challenges.

LinkedIn's Disruption of Traditional Résumés

Launched in May 2003, LinkedIn reshaped professional identity by transforming résumés into living profiles. Unlike static documents stored in desk drawers, LinkedIn profiles existed permanently in the digital sphere, visible, searchable and structured for recruiter access.

LinkedIn addressed a fundamental hiring problem: résumé inconsistency. Before LinkedIn, recruiters faced a challenge: no two résumés followed the same structure. By standardizing professional information into structured fields – experience, education, skills and recommendations – LinkedIn created a universally recognized professional language that everyone spoke.

As LinkedIn's user base expanded, from 10 million users in 2007 to over 100 million by 2011, having a profile became an essential career tool. By 2009, nearly half of hiring managers considered a missing LinkedIn profile a red flag. Beyond visibility, LinkedIn introduced peer validation. Features like recommendations and skill endorsements turned credibility into a public asset, replacing private reference checks with permanent, searchable testimonials.

By the 2010s, LinkedIn Recruiter allowed hiring teams to actively search for talent, rather than waiting for applications. By 2013, 93% of recruiters were sourcing candidates through LinkedIn, reducing the résumé's role as the primary hiring tool. For professionals, optimizing a LinkedIn profile became as crucial as crafting a résumé.

Visibility in recruiter searches depended on algorithm-driven ranking. By 2018, LinkedIn, with over 575 million users, established itself as the dominant professional network.

For many, particularly in technology, finance and corporate sectors, the LinkedIn profile had effectively replaced the traditional résumé. While résumés remained relevant for formal applications, they were no longer the primary gateway to opportunity; LinkedIn was.

The ATS Paradox: Efficiency vs. Exclusion

Originally designed to handle application overload, ATS has become a double-edged sword. By 2010, more than 75% of companies had adopted the ATS, and today virtually all Fortune 500 companies rely on them for recruitment.

ATS software parses résumés into structured data, allowing recruiters to search, rank and filter candidates. However, ATS has significant flaws that have been widely criticized. Keyword-matching, AI-driven ranking and knockout criteria automate selection but also introduce blind spots. These systems prioritize pattern-matching over potential, evaluating candidates based on rigid algorithms, rather than recognizing unconventional but highly capable individuals. Those with non-traditional career paths, such as freelancers, career changers or individuals with employment gaps, often find themselves filtered out, due to biases in system-driven screening methods.

Additionally, ATS has given rise to résumé-keyword manipulation, where candidates strategically insert job-description keywords to improve their rankings, sometimes outperforming genuinely qualified applicants.

Formatting poses another major issue, as a 2019 Jobscan study found that 98% of Fortune 500 ATS platforms misinterpret résumés containing tables, columns or graphics, leading to qualified candidates being overlooked.

A 2016 CareerBuilder study found that 75% of hiring managers admitted ATS had mistakenly rejected qualified applicants. Similarly, a 2018 Harvard Business School report estimated that 27 million workers were invisible to employers due to rigid ATS screening.

Ironically, while ATS was designed to improve hiring efficiency, it has made it more technical and exclusionary. Many companies now recognize that ATS has limitations and are exploring alternatives. Emerging intelligent hiring tools focus on skills, adaptability and problem-solving ability, rather than rigid keyword matching. This shift signals a potential decline in the résumé's dominance in hiring practices.

The Beginning of the End for the Résumé?

The historical evolution of the résumé – from hand-written letters to digital, AI-filtered applications – highlights its resilience. Despite its limitations and inefficiencies, the résumé has prevailed for over a century as a standard hiring tool.

However, the modern job market is evolving beyond the traditional résumé. As AI-driven hiring, skills-based assessments and digital professional branding take center stage, the résumé is increasingly becoming a secondary tool, rather than the primary determinant of hiring decisions. The question is no longer whether the résumé is flawed, it is how long it will remain relevant in a world where hiring is shifting toward automation-first recruitment strategies.

With artificial intelligence, predictive hiring models and machine-led candidate-discovery systems becoming mainstream, we will further explore how AI is fundamentally altering the hiring framework, shaping a future where résumés may no longer be necessary.

2.
The AI Revolution Begins

AI's Disruption of Traditional Recruitment

Artificial intelligence has upended traditional recruitment in ways that were unimaginable just a decade ago. What once required teams of recruiters manually sifting through stacks of documents has transformed into sophisticated systems capable of scanning thousands of applicants within seconds. This technological revolution isn't simply automating old processes, it's completely reimagining how companies identify, evaluate and select talent.

The first major breakthrough in AI-driven hiring came with résumé-screening automation. Early tools were little more than basic keyword scanners, but today's AI-powered systems analyze applications with far greater sophistication. Modern screening tools use machine learning algorithms to understand context beyond keyword matching, recognize transferable skills and predict job compatibility.

A key breakthrough lies in *natural language processing*

(NLP), a branch of AI that enables recruitment tools to analyze and interpret language like a human would. This allows job-search platforms to understand synonyms, implied meanings and context, rather than relying on exact keyword matches. As an example, an AI-powered system can recognize that someone applying for *"coding jobs"* may qualify for roles titled *"software engineer"* or *"developer"*, even if they didn't use the exact phrasing. It can identify hidden talent by evaluating real skills over résumé formatting or keyword manipulation.

While AI offers unparalleled efficiency, its true value lies in its ability to go beyond traditional résumés and uncover candidates with high potential, even if their background does not fit conventional hiring models. Companies leveraging smart recruitment platforms are discovering hidden talent pools, making hiring more data-driven, fair and efficient than ever before.

Predictive Hiring: A Next-Gen Shift in Talent Selection
Predictive hiring represents a fundamental shift in how organizations identify and select talent, redefining how they assess potential, shifting the focus from past

experience to future performance. Instead of relying on credentials and subjective interviews, data-driven models analyze behavioral patterns, work history and skills to forecast job success. This approach transforms hiring from a backward-looking process, focused on credentials, to a forward-looking system centered on potential and fit. Unlike traditional methods, which often favor linear career paths, this approach broadens access to talent by evaluating adaptability, problem-solving ability and learning potential – qualities that static documents rarely capture.

The first essential component of predictive hiring systems is sophisticated data collection and analysis. These systems gather information from multiple sources to build comprehensive candidate profiles. Beyond résumé data, they incorporate assessment results, digital footprints, work samples and even communication patterns during the application process.

The second key component involves performance prediction models, which use machine learning algorithms to identify patterns associated with success in specific roles. These models analyze historical data about employee performance, to determine which candidate characteristics best predict future outcomes.

The third component of advanced predictive hiring systems is behavioral assessment algorithms, which evaluate how candidates are likely to act in workplace situations. These algorithms analyze responses to scenario-based questions, simulation exercises, and even facial expressions and voice patterns during video interviews, to predict behavioral tendencies.

The fourth component focuses on cultural-fit evaluation, which predicts how well candidates will align with an organization's values and work environment. These systems analyze communication styles, work preferences and value indicators to forecast cultural alignment.

Real-world implementations of predictive hiring systems have delivered measurable improvements across multiple metrics. Organizations that have implemented predictive hiring tools report measurable improvements in hiring efficiency, candidate success rates and cost savings. These systems have been shown to increase diversity in hiring pools, improve new hire performance and reduce turnover, by identifying candidates with stronger long-term potential. Additionally, hiring timelines have shortened, and employers have observed higher satisfaction rates among hiring managers, due to more accurate candidate-job matches.

Despite these impressive outcomes, predictive hiring systems face important challenges. Algorithmic bias represents one of the most serious concerns, as these systems can inadvertently perpetuate historical hiring patterns that disadvantage certain groups.

One of the most well-known cases of AI bias in hiring involved Amazon's 2014 AI-powered hiring tool. By 2015, the company discovered that the system was biased against female candidates for technical roles. This happened because the AI had been trained on historical hiring data, which reflected male dominance in the tech industry. As a result, the algorithm downgraded résumés containing words like *"women's"* (e.g., *"women's chess club captain"*). It automatically penalized graduates from women's colleges. Amazon eventually scrapped the system after discovering that the AI was reinforcing – not eliminating – gender bias (*Reuters*, 2018). This case underscores a crucial point: AI models reflect the biases in the data they are trained on.

To mitigate the bias, leading predictive hiring platforms now implement several strategies:

1. Regular audits of machine learning models, to identify and correct unfair prediction patterns.
2. Diverse training data sets that include successful employees from different backgrounds.
3. Blind assessment techniques; personal information (e.g., gender, age, race) is removed from candidate profiles before evaluation.
4. Validation studies, to ensure predictions don't disadvantage protected groups.

Data privacy presents another significant concern. Predictive hiring systems collect substantial information about candidates, raising questions about consent, data security and appropriate use limitations. Leading providers address these concerns through clear privacy policies, data minimization practices, and compliance with regulations like the General Data Protection Regulation (GDPR) and the California Consumer Privacy Act (CCPA).

In my final analysis, predictive hiring works best as a decision-support tool rather than a replacement for human judgment. Companies that lean too heavily on machine-generated recommendations may overlook candidates with unique strengths that fall outside standard training data.

The ideal hiring processes should combine AI's data-driven insights, to streamline candidate evaluation and human intuition, to assess soft skills, motivation and cultural fit.

As AI hiring technology continues to evolve and refine itself, predictive hiring models and AI-powered talent discovery are shaping the future of recruitment.

Skills Over Credentials: The New Hiring Standard

The traditional emphasis on credentials is giving way to a more practical focus on skills and competencies, creating a fundamental shift in how companies evaluate talent. This transformation isn't happening in isolation; it's the result of several converging forces reshaping our understanding of what makes someone qualified for a job. For decades, degrees and certifications served as convenient proxies for ability, but today's employers are discovering that what someone can actually do matters more than the credentials they've collected.

Technology companies were among the first to break away from rigid credential requirements. For example, many companies publicly state that practical problem-solving ability, hands-on experience and technical knowledge often outweigh formal degrees.

The rapid pace of technological change has made continuous learning more valuable than static credentials. In fields like software development, data science and digital marketing, skills evolve faster than traditional degrees can keep up with. A Computer Science graduate from four years ago may already lack industry-relevant expertise, while a self-taught professional with hands-on experience or recent online training may possess more applicable skills.

Instead of relying on traditional degrees, companies now look for proof of real-world abilities, such as online portfolios showcasing past projects, open-source contributions or industry engagement, participation in hackathons, and skill-based certifications from Google, LinkedIn and other reputable platforms.

The impact of skills-based hiring on diversity and inclusion has been particularly notable. Credential requirements often reinforce social and economic barriers, limiting opportunities for candidates who may have the right skills but lack formal degrees. Competency-driven hiring expands access to talent from underrepresented backgrounds, allowing employers to broaden their workforce and improve diversity. Many organizations adopting skills assessments report increased diversity in technical hires, as hiring decisions become more data-driven and less reliant on traditional qualifications. By evaluating candidates based on demonstrated competencies, employers can identify high-potential talent from a wider range of socioeconomic, educational and cultural backgrounds.

As skills-based hiring continues to gain traction, companies are discovering that this approach not only enhances diversity but also leads to stronger, more adaptable workforces, equipped to meet the demands of an evolving job market.

For job-seekers navigating this new terrain, the shift toward competency-driven hiring creates both challenges and opportunities. The most successful candidates prioritize building and demonstrating relevant skills rather than simply accumulating qualifications. As more and more organizations continue adopting talent-focused recruitment, the traditional résumé is losing its relevance, further reinforcing the need for AI-driven hiring processes and methodologies.

Automated Candidate Discovery: The Shift from Reactive to Proactive Hiring

Automated candidate discovery systems have transformed how companies find talent, shifting from reactive job postings to proactive talent identification. These sophisticated platforms use artificial intelligence and data analytics to scan the digital domain for qualified professionals, often before they've even considered applying. The technology represents a fundamental change in recruitment strategy, from waiting for the right candidates to actively seeking them out.

AI-powered talent-mapping forms the foundation of modern candidate discovery. These systems create comprehensive maps of available talent across industries, specializations and geographic regions. Unlike traditional databases that simply store information, talent maps reveal relationships between skills, career progressions and hidden talent pools.

Social media analysis represents another powerful component of candidate discovery systems. These tools scan public social profiles across platforms like LinkedIn, Twitter, GitHub, Behance, Medium and industry-specific forums, to identify professionals demonstrating relevant expertise. This shift reinforces the importance of professional branding; candidates who actively showcase their skills online gain higher visibility in intelligent hiring environments.

While LinkedIn Recruiter pioneered this approach, newer, algorithm-enhanced platforms have expanded its capabilities, using network analysis to uncover qualified candidates who might not surface in traditional keyword-based searches.

Beyond professional networks, digital-footprint evaluation provides a broader view of a candidate's expertise, interests and professional engagement. These systems analyze publicly-available content, such as industry contributions, thought leadership and participation in relevant discussions, to assess cultural alignment and potential fit. These systems excel at identifying passive candidates: professionals not actively seeking new positions but potentially open to the right opportunity. Traditional recruitment methods miss this talent pool entirely, which represents roughly 70% of the workforce, according to LinkedIn data.

Automated discovery systems also evaluate potential fit between candidates and organizations. Rather than relying on subjective impressions, these platforms use data to predict alignment across multiple dimensions. Cultural-fit assessments have become increasingly sophisticated, with some systems analyzing writing samples, social media activity and other digital content, to create personality profiles that predict alignment with company values and work environments. Such approaches aim to reduce early-stage turnover, by identifying candidates whose communication styles and work preferences match team dynamics.

The scalability of advanced talent-sourcing systems represents a major advantage over traditional recruitment methods. As these systems continue to evolve, they're incorporating more sophisticated data sources and analytical techniques. The next generation of platforms is beginning to analyze video content, professional webinars and even voice patterns from podcast appearances, to identify expertise and communication styles.

The hiring revolution is no longer a question of if; it's a matter of when. The future isn't waiting, and neither should we.

3.
New Ways to Shine

Asynchronous Video Interviews

Asynchronous video interviews represent a fundamental shift in how companies evaluate talent. Unlike traditional methods, asynchronous interviews allow candidates to record responses to predetermined questions at their convenience.

This innovation emerged around 2015, as organizations sought more efficient ways to screen candidates, while reducing scheduling conflicts and geographical limitations. Pioneering companies like HireVue (founded in 2004), VidCruiter (founded in 2009) and Spark Hire (founded in 2012) developed platforms that have since become integral across various industries, from retail to finance.

The beauty of asynchronous video interviews lies in their flexibility. Recruiters can send interview requests to dozens of candidates simultaneously, who then have a window of typically forty-eight to seventy-two hours to record their responses. This eliminates the scheduling gymnastics that plague traditional hiring processes. A recruiter in New York can evaluate candidates from Singapore, São Paulo and Stockholm without anyone adjusting their sleep schedule. For candidates, this means preparing and recording answers when they feel most confident, rather than rushing from another commitment to make an interview slot.

Standardization represents another key advantage. Every candidate receives identical questions in the same order, creating a level playing field for comparison. This consistency helps hiring teams make more objective evaluations, since they can directly compare how different candidates approach the same challenges. Questions typically follow a structured format, often beginning with basic introductions before progressing to behavioral scenarios, technical knowledge assessments and situational judgment tests.

The AI analysis capabilities of modern platforms add another dimension to these interviews. Advanced algorithms can evaluate not just what candidates say, but how they say it. These systems analyze facial expressions, voice tone, word choice and even micro-expressions, to assess confidence, emotional intelligence and authenticity. Some platforms can generate personality profiles, predict job performance and flag potential concerns based on these analyses.

Global accessibility has made asynchronous interviews particularly valuable for multinational corporations and remote-first companies. A candidate needs only a smartphone or a computer with a camera to participate, opening opportunities to talent pools previously excluded by geography or economic barriers. This worldwide reach helps companies build diverse teams across cultural and national boundaries, without the expense of flying candidates to headquarters.

The technical infrastructure supporting these interviews has matured rapidly. Modern platforms now offer a suite of sophisticated features designed to streamline the hiring process. These include customizable question sets tailored to specific roles, predefined time limits for candidate responses, intuitive review dashboards for evaluators, and comprehensive candidate-management tools, which facilitate seamless tracking and communication throughout the recruitment journey. Such advancements have democratized access to cutting-edge recruitment technologies, enabling organizations of varying sizes to implement solutions that best fit their unique needs and resources.

For optimal recording quality, candidates should find well-lit, quiet environments with neutral backgrounds. Most platforms recommend wired internet connections rather than wi-fi, to prevent disruptions. Candidates typically get one or two practice questions to test their equipment before the actual interview begins. Once started, candidates usually have a set time to prepare (thirty to sixty seconds) and a maximum time to respond (usually one to three minutes) for each question.

Question formats vary widely, but generally fall into several categories. Behavioral questions *("Tell me about a time when...")* assess past experiences, problem-solving abilities and the candidate's mindset, initiative and approach to challenges. Situational questions *("What would you do if...")* evaluate judgment, decision-making, adaptability, strategic thinking and the ability to perform under pressure. Technical questions test specific knowledge relevant to the role. Cultural-fit questions gauge alignment with company values. Most interviews include five to seven questions and take fifteen to thirty minutes to complete.

The AI evaluation metrics used by advanced platforms are surprisingly granular. Beyond basic speech recognition, these systems analyze linguistic patterns, including word choice, speech rate, filler words and sentence complexity. Facial analysis tracks expressions, eye contact and engagement levels. Some platforms even measure candidate honesty by detecting inconsistencies between verbal and non-verbal cues. These metrics generate scores across dimensions like communication skills, emotional intelligence and problem-solving ability.

Unilever[1] provides a compelling example of successful, AI-driven recruitment implementation. By integrating artificial intelligence into their hiring process, they achieved a 75% reduction in recruitment time, decreasing from four months to four weeks. This innovation also led to significant efficiency gains, saving over fifty thousand hours of interviewer time annually. The company's candidate pool became more diverse, expanding hires from

---

[1] Source: *"The Practical Application of AI: Unilever Reduced Recruitment Time by 75%."* PUMPedu, (2023).

2,600 universities, compared to their previous reach of 840 institutions. Additionally, candidate satisfaction scores improved by 16%, with applicants appreciating the flexibility and modern approach facilitated by AI integration.

A leading global investment bank transformed its campus recruiting by implementing asynchronous interviews. They expanded outreach to 40% more universities, and doubled the number of candidates interviewed in first rounds. The initiative improved inclusivity, resulting in a 27% increase in female hires and a notable rise in representation from underrepresented groups.

A major retail employer leveraged asynchronous video interviews to manage seasonal hiring surges. With over 1.2 million applications processed, they reduced time-to-hire by 34% and saved approximately $1 million annually in recruitment costs. Hiring managers reported better candidate quality at final interview stages, leading to improved retention.

Despite these successes, asynchronous video interviews come with limitations. Technology barriers remain significant for candidates without reliable internet access or updated devices. Some applicants, particularly in rural areas or developing regions, may be excluded from opportunities due to these technical requirements. Companies must consider providing alternatives or accommodations to maintain equitable hiring practices.

The lack of personal connection presents another challenge. The rapport-building that naturally occurs in live conversations is absent in asynchronous formats. Candidates can't read the room, adjust their approach based on interviewer reactions, or ask clarifying questions. This one-way communication can feel impersonal, and may disadvantage candidates whose strengths lie in interpersonal dynamics rather than prepared presentations.

AI evaluation systems face ongoing scrutiny regarding bias. Early algorithms showed preferences for certain speech patterns, facial expressions and communication styles that correlated with specific demographic groups. A research analysis carried out a few years ago found that some systems gave lower scores to candidates with accents or non-Western facial expressions. Leading platforms now implement regular bias audits and algorithm adjustments, but concerns persist about whether these systems truly provide fair assessment across diverse candidate pools.

Privacy issues also loom large. Candidates often wonder what happens to their video data after the hiring process concludes. Who owns these recordings? How long are they stored? Could they be used for purposes beyond the specific job application? The legal framework around this data remains underdeveloped in many jurisdictions, creating uncertainty for both companies and candidates.

Lights, Camera, You're Hired!

For job-seekers facing asynchronous interviews, preparation remains key. Start by researching the company thoroughly and understanding the role requirements. Practice recording yourself answering common interview questions, to become comfortable with the format. Pay attention to your environment; choose a clean, well-lit space with minimal distractions, and test your equipment before the actual interview.

When recording responses, speak clearly and maintain eye contact with the camera. For behavioral questions, structure your response into clear, manageable segments; this not only enhances clarity, but also helps you recall each part of your answer with greater ease and confidence. Keep responses concise but complete, typically aiming for sixty to ninety seconds per question. Show enthusiasm through vocal variety and appropriate facial expressions, as these non-verbal cues significantly impact the AI evaluation. During the interview, make a conscious effort to mentally note – or briefly jot down – the questions asked, as this will allow you to reference them meaningfully in your follow-up communication, discussed below.

Dress professionally, as you would for an in-person interview, even if recording from home. Many candidates make the mistake of dressing too casually, which can create a negative impression. Remember that first impressions, visually and verbally, form quickly, so the opening seconds of each response matter tremendously.

After completing the interview, follow up with a thoughtfully crafted thank-you email to the interviewer, a practice I've discussed in detail in my book *Find the Ladder*. Reference specific questions from the asynchronous interview to demonstrate your engagement and cognitive presence; this personal touch can help bridge the connection gap inherent in the asynchronous format.

Companies implementing these systems should provide clear instructions and reasonable flexibility for candidates with disabilities or technical limitations. Transparency about how videos will be evaluated, stored and protected helps build mutual trust. The most effective hiring programs use asynchronous interviews as one component of a multi-stage process, rather than the sole evaluation method.

As technology continues advancing, asynchronous video interviews will likely incorporate more interactive elements while maintaining their convenience advantages. Some platforms already experiment with branching scenarios, where candidate responses determine subsequent questions, creating a more personalized experience while preserving the asynchronous benefits.

The Future of Digital Professional Profiles

The static professional profile is rapidly becoming a relic of the past. While LinkedIn revolutionized how we present ourselves professionally online, today's digital scenario demands more dynamic and interactive ways to showcase skills and experience. The next generation of professional profiles is emerging: living, breathing digital entities, which demonstrate capabilities rather than merely listing them.

Traditional, text-based profiles struggle to capture the full scope of professional abilities. They *tell* rather than *show*, creating a fundamental disconnect between claimed skills and actual capabilities. This gap has driven the evolution toward interactive portfolios, where professionals can demonstrate their expertise through tangible examples, communication styles and real-time projects.

Interactive skill demonstrations represent the cornerstone of modern professional profiles. Rather than simply claiming proficiency in data analysis, professionals now embed interactive dashboards they've created, allowing profile visitors to manipulate variables and see analytical thinking in action. Designers showcase interactive prototypes rather than static images. Programmers include code snippets with live execution environments, where visitors can modify parameters and observe results. These demonstrations transform passive claims into active proof, giving recruiters and potential employers direct insight into the candidate's capabilities.

Real-time project showcases elevate the concept of professional representation by offering a living testament to ongoing work and evolving expertise. Instead of listing past accomplishments in static form, individuals now weave their current undertakings into their professional narrative. Developers may display live-code contributions, while the creative ones seamlessly stream their latest articles, podcasts or video content into curated profiles. Project leaders, too, present dynamic workflow snapshots – such as anonymized task boards or collaborative frameworks – which reflect how they think, plan and execute in real time. This unfolding window into one's present capabilities and work style offers a depth of insight that traditional résumés could never attain.

Verified credentials have become essential as digital profiles evolve. The problem of credential inflation – where candidates exaggerate qualifications – has plagued hiring for decades. Modern profiles address this through third-party verification systems. Educational institutions now issue digital credentials directly to graduate profiles. Professional certifications appear with blockchain-verified timestamps and expiration dates. Previous employers confirm tenure and responsibilities through digital attestations. These verification mechanisms build trust in ways paper résumés never could.

AI-powered skill-mapping represents perhaps the most transformative element of next-generation profiles. Advanced algorithms analyze work samples, contributions and digital footprints, to identify skills the professional may not even realize they possess. These systems create comprehensive skill graphs, showing not just what someone knows, but how their skills interconnect and which adjacent capabilities they could easily develop. For job-seekers, this provides clarity on positioning; for employers, it reveals hidden potential that traditional screening might miss.

Blockchain technology has emerged as a powerful tool for experience verification. Unlike traditional references that require phone calls or emails, blockchain-verified experience creates immutable records of professional history. Smart contracts automatically verify project completion, with stakeholders digitally signing off on contributions. This creates an unbroken chain of professional activity that cannot be falsified or exaggerated. For professionals with unconventional career paths or freelance backgrounds, these verified records provide credibility that traditional employment verification cannot match.

The visual presentation of professional information has also transformed dramatically. Augmented-reality (AR) portfolio presentations allow creative professionals to showcase their work in three-dimensional space. Architects can present building designs that viewers can walk through virtually. Product designers demonstrate prototypes that can be examined from all angles. Even data analysts use AR to present multi-dimensional visualizations, which reveal patterns invisible in flat presentations. These immersive experiences create memorable impressions that flat portfolios cannot achieve.

Virtual reality (VR) takes this immersion further, enabling professionals to create entire environments showcasing their work. Software engineers build virtual coding spaces, where visitors can see complex systems visualized in three dimensions. Teachers create virtual classrooms demonstrating their instructional techniques. Healthcare professionals simulate patient interactions. In clinical training, VR is used to rehearse surgical procedures or emergency scenarios in highly realistic environments, enhancing both precision and preparedness. These VR experiences provide context and depth that traditional portfolios lack, allowing professionals to demonstrate not just what they've done but how they work.

Digital badges and certifications have evolved from simple icons to rich information sources. Modern badges contain metadata about the skills they represent, assessment methods used and difficulty level. They link to actual work samples demonstrating the certified skill in action. Micro-credentials stack together to show specialization depth, while breadth badges illustrate versatility. This granular approach to certification allows professionals to precisely document capabilities, in ways degrees and traditional certifications cannot.

Social-proof algorithms now analyze professional networks to identify authentic expertise. These systems examine not just connection quantity, but quality and context. They identify which professionals others in their field consistently turn to for advice. They analyze conversation patterns, to determine thought leadership in specific domains. They evaluate engagement with content to assess impact. These algorithms create reputation scores based on actual professional influence rather than self-promotion, providing objective measures of standing within professional communities.

And, as a gentle tip, if a platform like LinkedIn prompts you to share your perspective on a topic related to your expertise, don't ignore it; these small signals can significantly boost your visibility in ways that matter.

Professional reputation scoring has matured beyond simple endorsements. Modern systems analyze the weight of who is doing the endorsing, creating weighted reputation graphs. They track how recommendations flow through professional networks, identifying trusted nodes. They analyze work quality through peer reviews and client feedback. These sophisticated reputation mechanisms create multi-dimensional pictures of professional standing that simple testimonials never could.

Building a future-ready digital presence begins with strategic platform selection. While LinkedIn remains the foundation, professionals now cultivate visibility across specialized platforms. Technical professionals showcase work on GitHub, designers on Behance, writers on Medium and visual creators on Instagram. The key lies in crafting a cohesive cross-platform identity, where each outlet highlights distinct facets of professional capability, all while maintaining a consistent and recognizable personal brand.

Content curation has become essential as profiles grow more dynamic. Professionals must carefully select which projects to highlight, which skills to demonstrate and which credentials to emphasize. The most effective profiles tell coherent professional stories, with each element reinforcing a central narrative about capabilities and specialization. This curation requires regular pruning as careers evolve, removing outdated information and highlighting new capabilities.

Digital branding principles have evolved beyond basic consistency. Modern professional brands incorporate personal values and working styles alongside skills and experience. They highlight collaboration approaches, problem-solving methodologies and ethical frameworks. This holistic presentation helps potential employers and collaborators assess not just capability but fit, reducing mismatches that lead to failed professional relationships.

Network-building approaches now focus primarily on quality. Rather than accumulating connections, professionals cultivate meaningful relationships with strategic collaborators, mentors and industry peers. They engage in knowledge exchange through content creation and curation. They participate in professional communities, contributing expertise rather than simply networking. These authentic relationships create stronger professional ecosystems than transactional networking ever could.

Looking forward, professional profiles will likely become even more interactive and verification-focused. Experts predict the rise of skill simulations, where professionals complete standardized challenges in virtual environments, creating comparable measures of capability. Continuous assessment will likely replace point-in-time certifications, with profiles showing skill-development trajectories rather than static achievements. Reputation systems will grow increasingly sophisticated, incorporating more refined and layered measures of professional impact and influence.

The boundaries between profiles and portfolios will continue to blur. Static information will give way entirely to dynamic demonstrations. Verification will become the norm rather than the exception. Most importantly, professional identity will shift from backward-looking documentation to forward-facing capability demonstration, focusing less on where someone has been, and more on what they can do now and learn in future.

Hiring Through Play: Gamified Recruitment

Recruitment has undergone a remarkable transformation, with the introduction of game elements into what was once a formal, rigid and often stressful process. Companies now incorporate interactive challenges, simulations and competitive elements, to evaluate candidates in ways that traditional interviews simply cannot. This approach, known as gamified recruitment, creates an environment where candidates can demonstrate their abilities through engaging activities rather than just talking about them.

One prominent example of this approach involves the use of neuroscience-inspired games to evaluate cognitive and emotional attributes. These short, interactive assessments measure traits such as attention to detail, risk tolerance, learning agility and decision-making patterns. Rather than relying on rehearsed interview answers or keyword-stuffed résumés, these tools reveal how candidates naturally think and respond under varying conditions. Typically completed in under thirty minutes, the games generate valuable data, which offers a deeper understanding of an individual's potential fit for specific roles.

Skill-based challenges form the foundation of many gamified hiring systems. Unlike traditional technical assessments, which often feel like exams, these challenges immerse candidates in realistic scenarios. Software developers might debug code in a game-like interface, where they earn points for efficient solutions. Graphic designers might participate in timed design challenges with specific constraints, mimicking real project conditions. Financial analysts might work through data puzzles that reflect actual monetary problems. These challenges reveal not just technical proficiency but also how candidates approach problems under pressure.

Problem-solving scenarios take this concept further by presenting candidates with complex, interactive situations that have no single correct answer. They include digital assessments with interactive video scenarios where candidates make decisions as events unfold, revealing their judgment and reasoning. These scenarios often include unexpected complications or resource constraints, testing adaptability and agility. The game-like format encourages authentic responses rather than rehearsed answers, giving employers insight into genuine problem-solving approaches.

In addition to problem-solving tasks, personality assessment games offer an innovative alternative to standard personality questionnaires. Rather than asking direct questions about work preferences, these games observe behavior in simulated environments, in order to infer personality traits and cognitive abilities. As an example, certain games place candidates in roles such as restaurant servers managing multiple tasks, tracking numerous behavioral data points, from task prioritization to responses under pressure. These insights assist employers in matching candidates to roles where their innate tendencies align with job requirements, enhancing the likelihood of success and job satisfaction.

Team collaboration simulations address a critical hiring need: assessing how candidates work with others. These multiplayer games place candidates in virtual teams, tackling challenges that require communication and coordination. They contain simulations, where candidates must collaborate to solve puzzles or complete projects. These games reveal leadership tendencies, communication styles and conflict resolution approaches in a natural context, providing information that's nearly impossible to gather in traditional interviews.

The technology sector has embraced gamified hiring with particular enthusiasm, using interactive platforms, where programmers solve logic-based challenges under time constraints. Competitive leaderboards often accompany these puzzles, turning routine assessments into spirited contests. What might otherwise be a sterile testing experience becomes an engaging intellectual competition that many developers actively enjoy.

Consulting firms have adopted business simulations that mirror the complex problems their consultants often face. These virtual environments challenge candidates to analyze data, formulate strategies, and present reasoned recommendations for hypothetical corporate dilemmas. In some cases, applicants must manage simulated cities or companies, balancing limited resources against multiple stakeholder demands. These experiences not only assess analytical thinking, business acumen and commercial awareness, but also reveal how candidates structure decisions under pressure.

Retail organizations use customer-service scenarios to identify candidates with the right temperament and skills for customer-facing roles. Candidates may be placed in realistic virtual environments – such as bustling storefronts or fast-paced service scenarios – where they must manage customer interactions, prioritize competing tasks and resolve conflicts. These simulations measure patience, empathy, adaptability and practical problem-solving, helping to identify individuals who will thrive under real-world retail pressures.

The psychological principles behind gamification in hiring are well-established. First, games trigger intrinsic motivation: the desire to engage in an activity for its own sake rather than external rewards. This motivation leads candidates to invest more effort and show more authentic behavior than in traditional assessments, where they're consciously trying to impress evaluators. The flow state that well-designed games can induce – where someone is fully immersed in an engaging challenge – reveals how candidates perform when they're at their best.

Gamified hiring transforms recruitment into a more relaxed and revealing process. The playful format eases candidate stress, shifting focus from self-presentation to task performance. This reduction in pressure often allows individuals to display their true abilities, especially those who struggle in traditional interview settings.

Perhaps most importantly, games allow for natural behavior observation. When candidates are engaged in solving a puzzle or managing a simulation, they display authentic decision-making patterns and interpersonal tendencies. For those with strong practical skills but weaker verbal articulation, these tasks offer a rare chance to show rather than tell. This authenticity enables recruiters to make better matches between candidates and roles, reducing turnover and improving future performance.

To perform well, candidates should approach these assessments with authenticity, resisting the urge to overthink or deliver what seems like the "right" response. Practicing similar games, managing time wisely and carefully reading instructions can improve performance. Whether it's logic-based tasks or business simulations, understanding the underlying competencies being tested is key.

The rise of gamified hiring represents a win-win evolution in recruitment. Employers gain deeper insight into candidates' actual abilities and work tendencies, while candidates enjoy a more engaging process that often feels fairer than traditional methods. As these technologies continue to develop, we can expect even more sophisticated simulations that blur the line between assessment and actual work, creating hiring experiences that truly preview the job itself.

AI-Driven Skill-Assessment Platforms

Intelligent assessment platforms are gradually revolutionizing how companies evaluate talent, moving far beyond the limitations of résumé scanning. These sophisticated systems can now measure not just what you claim to know, but what you can actually do, and even predict how you might perform in specific roles. Unlike traditional assessments, which test memorized knowledge, AI platforms analyze how candidates solve problems, communicate ideas and approach challenges in real time. The technology powering these platforms combines several advanced capabilities that work together, to create a comprehensive picture of a candidate's abilities.

Natural language processing (NLP) examines written and verbal communication. When candidates respond to questions or complete writing tasks, NLP algorithms analyze factors like vocabulary usage, sentence structure and communication clarity. They can identify whether someone communicates concisely or tends toward verbosity, if they adjust their tone appropriately for different contexts, and even assess their ability to explain complex concepts in accessible ways.

In the sections that follow, we'll briefly explore seven core dimensions that define AI-driven assessments, each offering a distinct lens into how candidates think, behave, adapt and perform. From pattern recognition and behavioral modeling to cognitive tests and cultural alignment, these components collectively create a multi-layered understanding of human potential.

Pattern-recognition algorithms observe how candidates tackle problems, identifying approaches that correlate with success in specific roles. These patterns reveal cognitive style: methodical, intuitive, exploratory or cautious; insights that help match individuals to roles where their natural approaches are strengths.

Behavioral modeling further refines candidate profiles by evaluating how individuals respond to workplace simulations. Factors like speed, consistency, adaptability and interpersonal tone are captured, providing rich data on how someone might perform under pressure, manage conflict or adapt to changing priorities.

Predictive performance modeling ties these elements together, using historical benchmarks to forecast job success. As more data is processed, the accuracy of these predictions improves, helping employers anticipate not just fit, but also future performance.

Technical-skill evaluations represent the most straightforward application of AI assessment platforms. Programming assessments analyze code quality, structure and problem-solving logic. Data-science tasks test statistical fluency, analytical thinking and the ability to extract insights from complex datasets. Rather than checking for memorized knowledge, these tools assess real-world competence.

Soft-skill measurements present a more complex challenge, which AI platforms are increasingly equipped to handle. In one common assessment type, candidates respond to video scenarios showing workplace conflicts or customer interactions; AI analyzes their verbal responses, facial expressions and proposed solutions, to gauge interpersonal skills. These assessments reveal traits like empathy, good listening, resilience and collaboration style.

Cognitive-ability tests measure how candidates process information, learn new concepts and solve abstract problems. Modern AI versions of these assessments adapt in real-time based on performance, presenting increasingly difficult challenges as candidates demonstrate mastery. This adaptive approach provides more precise measurement while reducing test anxiety. These assessments help identify candidates who can learn quickly and think flexibly, regardless of their formal education or academic background.

Cultural-fit assessments examine alignment between a candidate's values, work-style preferences and motivational drivers, and an organization's culture and work environment. Some individuals flourish in flexible, purpose-driven roles, while others seek structure and achievement. Rather than promoting a one-size-fits-all profile, these tools emphasize alignment.

Preparing for AI assessments requires a shift in mindset. Authenticity matters more than perfection. Rather than rehearsing canned responses, candidates should familiarize themselves with different assessment formats, to become comfortable with the interfaces and question types. Understanding the intent behind each task helps tailor performance, while honest engagement typically yields the best results. Attempts to "game" the system often backfire, as inconsistencies are quickly flagged by the algorithms.

Candidates benefit from understanding how their results will be interpreted. Most AI assessment platforms measure multiple dimensions, rather than producing a single score: one test might assess collaboration, adaptability and emotional regulation; another might evaluate precision, speed and conceptual clarity. This breakdown provides feedback that can enhance future performance, even if a candidate isn't selected.

These multidimensional results provide valuable self-insight, regardless of hiring outcomes. Candidates who receive detailed feedback can identify personal strengths to emphasize in future applications, and areas for development.

For candidates, basic logistics also matter. A strong internet connection, a distraction-free space and clear understanding of instructions are crucial. Poor preparation on these fronts can result in underperformance, regardless of actual abilities.

The growing use of AI assessments raises important ethical considerations. Algorithmic bias represents a primary concern, as assessment systems trained on historical data may perpetuate existing workplace disparities. Responsible providers address this through regular bias audits and continuous monitoring of results across demographic groups.

The accessibility of AI assessments for candidates with disabilities presents another ethical dimension. While some platforms offer flexibilities like extended time or alternative formats, others may inadvertently disadvantage candidates with certain disabilities. Companies committed to inclusive hiring ensure their assessment platforms accommodate diverse needs and provide alternative evaluation methods when necessary.

4.
Mastering the Future

Building Your AI-Proof Digital Presence

With the sweeping rise of AI poised to redefine the future of hiring, building a resilient online professional profile is no longer optional; it's imperative. This goes far beyond merely maintaining a professional LinkedIn profile or personal website. It involves constructing a strategic, dynamic identity that appeals to both intelligent screening tools and human recruiters alike. A truly AI-proof presence is built to navigate system-led screening while authentically showcasing your unique value proposition.

The shift toward AI-driven hiring has fundamentally changed the rules of job-seeking. Algorithms now scan, sort and rank candidates before human eyes ever see an application. These systems look for specific patterns, keywords and indicators of success, which may differ from what traditional hiring managers prioritized. Establishing a future-focused online identity means understanding these new rules and strategically positioning yourself to thrive within them.

Think of your digital presence as a constellation of touch-points across the internet; each element – your social profiles, portfolio sites, published content and digital footprint – contributes to a complete picture, which both algorithmic screening technologies and human recruiters use to evaluate your fit for opportunities. The goal isn't to game the system, but to authentically present your skills and experiences in ways that modern hiring technologies can properly interpret and value.

What follows is a structured, step-by-step exploration of the core elements that define a future-ready online footprint, designed to equip you with the clarity, strategy and tools needed to thrive in the era of data-driven, technology-enhanced hiring.

Strategic keyword optimization begins with understanding how intelligent hiring platforms interpret your professional information. These systems scan for specific terms that indicate relevant skills, experiences and qualifications. Start by researching industry-specific terminology and the exact language used in job descriptions that interest you. Tools like LinkedIn's Skills

Assessments can help identify the most relevant keywords for your field. Create a master list of keywords that represent your core competencies, technical skills, soft skills and industry knowledge. Then, naturally incorporate these terms throughout your digital profiles, ensuring they appear in context rather than as obvious keyword stuffing. Remember that modern AI is sophisticated enough to understand semantic relationships, so using related terms and natural language works better than repetition.

To stand out in AI-augmented hiring systems, candidates must speak the evolving language of their industries. The following list offers a sample of advanced, forward-looking keyword phrases across ten distinct professional roles, specifically developed to align with modern algorithmic screening. These terms are not generic buzzwords, but rather context-rich descriptors that signal high competency and strategic relevance. While they may not be in everyday use, they are well understood by AI systems, and serve as powerful indicators of professional fluency in future-ready skills.

1. Technical Roles

For IT specialists, software engineers, developers, cloud architects, cybersecurity professionals, etc.

Example keyword phrases:
- *modular code architecture*
- *cloud-native orchestration*
- *asynchronous microservices*
- *Infrastructure as Code (IaC)*
- *full-stack solutioning*

2. Creative Roles

For content creators, designers, media professionals, brand strategists, marketers, etc.

Example keyword phrases:
- *cross-platform storytelling*
- *experiential content design*
- *narrative positioning*
- *visual identity refinement*
- *interactive media fluency*

3. Management Roles

For professionals in executive leadership, project management, team supervision, business operations, etc.

Example keyword phrases:
- *strategic vision implementation*
- *operational agility management*
- *outcome-focused governance*
- *change navigation strategy*
- *P-and-L-driven operational oversight*

4. *Analytical and Research Roles*

For professionals in data science, market research, policy, finance, healthcare analysis, academic research, etc.

Example keyword phrases:
- *inferential modeling*
- *data triangulation*
- *evidence synthesis*
- *hypothesis validation*
- *multivariate insight generation*

5. *AI and Emerging Tech Roles*

For professionals in artificial intelligence, machine learning, robotics, quantum computing, blockchain, innovation labs, etc.

Example keyword phrases:
- *neural architecture refinement*

- *ethical algorithm deployment*
- *model drift detection*
- *autonomous system calibration*
- *explainable AI development*

6. Marketing and Communications Roles

For digital marketers, brand strategists, growth hackers, marketing analysts, etc.

Example keyword phrases:
- *psychographic segmentation*
- *multichannel narrative attribution*
- *conversion funnel optimization*
- *viral loop mechanics*
- *brand resonance strategy*

7. Customer-centric and Client-Facing Roles

For professionals in customer service, business development, sales, support, client relations, etc.

Example keyword phrases:
- *CX journey mapping*
- *relationship lifecycle management*
- *needs-based consultative engagement*
- *service excellence design*

- *human-centered resolution*

8. Operational and Logistics Roles

For professionals in supply chain, procurement, logistics, facilities, manufacturing, etc.

Example keyword phrases:
- *lean throughput optimization*
- *resource orchestration*
- *capacity planning algorithms*
- *procurement lifecycle strategy*
- *logistics disruption mitigation*

9. Education, Learning and Training Roles

For teachers, corporate trainers, learning-and-development specialists, instructional designers, academic professionals, etc.

Example keyword phrases:
- *differentiated learning architecture*
- *adaptive curriculum structuring*
- *learner-centered content mapping*
- *guided cognitive development*
- *digital pedagogy integration*

10. Sustainability and Impact-Oriented Roles

For professionals in ESG (environmental, social, governance), sustainability strategy, nonprofit leadership, CSR, climate innovation, etc.

Example keyword phrases:
- *regenerative systems design*
- *carbon-footprint optimization*
- *stakeholder impact alignment*
- *circular economy integration*
- *ESG-aligned planning*

Since this book is rooted in future-focused hiring and digital evolution, the roles and refined keyword phrases outlined above are intentionally curated to reflect the emerging demands of tomorrow's workforce. By embedding such language authentically into your digital presence – across portfolios, profiles and professional summaries – you signal alignment with innovation, adaptability and relevance in a rapidly transforming job market. This isn't just about being seen by intelligent hiring engines; it's about being understood, noticed and selected.

Cross-platform consistency strengthens your digital

identity and helps AI systems connect your various online presences. While each platform has unique features and audiences, maintaining consistency in how you present your professional narrative is key. This doesn't mean identical content everywhere; it means ensuring your core professional story remains coherent across platforms.

Start with consistent naming. Use the same professional name across all platforms, making it easier for both AI and humans to connect your various profiles. Your professional headshot should be recent and recognizable across platforms, though it can be tailored to match each platform's culture (more formal for LinkedIn, perhaps more approachable for a personal website).

Your professional bio should maintain consistent themes while adapting to each platform's length requirements and audience expectations. Core elements like your professional focus, key skills and career highlights should align across platforms, even if the specific wording varies.

Most importantly, ensure your work history, education and major accomplishments match across platforms. Discrepancies in dates, job titles or achievements can raise red flags for both AI screening tools and human recruiters.

Digital portfolio development has become essential across nearly all industries, not just creative fields. A well-crafted portfolio provides concrete evidence of your capabilities that both AI and human evaluators can assess. The format will vary by profession – code repositories for developers, case studies for consultants, writing samples for content creators, project galleries for designers – but the principle remains the same: *show, don't just tell.*

When building your portfolio, focus on quality over quantity. Select projects that demonstrate range, your solutions-based mindset and measurable results. For each featured project, include context about the challenge addressed, your specific role, the approach taken and the outcomes achieved. Use metrics whenever possible: percentages, time saved, numerical improvements, or other quantifiable outcomes that help automation engines recognize your impact. Ensure that your portfolio is easily accessible from your other digital profiles, creating a seamless experience for anyone reviewing your credentials.

Contributing well-crafted articles related to your field of expertise, to professional platforms such as LinkedIn and Medium, enhances your credibility and signals proactive thought leadership. Equally important are peer endorsements and authentic recommendations, which serve as powerful social proof of your strengths and reinforce your professional reputation. The goal is to build a dynamic, living record of your professional identity, one that speaks on your behalf even when you're not actively pursuing new opportunities.

Participate meaningfully in industry-related communities. This might include contributing to open-source projects, answering questions on platforms such as Quora, or engaging in professionally moderated subreddits on the Reddit platform. These activities create digital breadcrumbs that reflect your expertise and proactive engagement within your professional sphere.

Self-Audit

Now let's move to practical exercises that will help you audit and enhance your current digital footprint.

Begin with a visibility audit worksheet. First, document all your existing professional profiles and content. List every platform, network, portfolio site or website where you have a professional presence. For each, note when it was last updated and evaluate its effectiveness, on a scale from one to ten.

Next, conduct a self-search. Use incognito or private-browsing mode to search your name online, along with relevant professional terms. Document what appears on the first two pages of results. Wear the hat of a recruiter or hiring manager and ask yourself: "Am I impressed?" Take note of any outdated or irrelevant results that need addressing.

Evaluate your keyword alignment by comparing the language in your profiles against five to ten job descriptions that interest you. Highlight recurring terms and concepts in the job descriptions, then check if these appear naturally in your profiles. Note gaps where important industry terms are missing from your digital presence.

Assess your visual brand consistency by placing screenshots of your various profiles side by side. Do they reflect a unified, coherent professional identity? Note inconsistencies in your photos, titles, messaging or visual presentation – any element that might create confusion or dilute your credibility.

One personal strategy I recommend from experience is what I call the "mind restart advantage". After your initial audit, take a minimum break of a day or two, then return to your profiles with a fresh perspective. You'll be surprised how clearly areas for improvement – or brilliant sections you hadn't fully appreciated before – reveal themselves when viewed through fresh eyes.

Finally, ask yourself, does your presence highlight your most marketable strengths? Are your most recent and relevant projects or achievements reflected? Is there a clear, accessible path between your profiles and portfolio? Identify anything that feels outdated or unclear, and make a plan to align it with your professional narrative.

Platform-specific optimization techniques vary based on each network's unique algorithms and audience expectations. On LinkedIn, complete every section of your profile thoughtfully, aiming for "All-Star" status. Use the headline field strategically; rather than listing only your current job title, highlight your core specialty and unique value proposition. The "About" section should narrate your professional story in a compelling manner, while seamlessly incorporating relevant industry keywords.

Consider adapting strong elements from your résumé, rephrased to suit the platform's tone and searchability.

LinkedIn's "Skills" section directly feeds into search algorithms, so select skills strategically based on your target roles. Regularly take skill assessments to earn verification badges. Request recommendations that specifically mention key skills you want to be found for.

For personal websites, ensure your site is mobile-responsive and loads quickly; AI crawlers and human recruiters alike will penalize slow or poorly functioning sites. Include a clear value proposition on your homepage, which states who you are, what you do and who you serve. Incorporate relevant keywords naturally in page titles, headings and content. Feature standout personal reviews, recommendations or professional testimonials prominently on the homepage, to build instant credibility. Include a dedicated projects or portfolio section, with detailed case studies.

Vary your content formats to showcase different skills. Written articles demonstrate communication skills and subject expertise. Video content shows presentation abilities and personality. Visual content, like infographics, displays your ability to simplify complex information. Interactive projects showcase technical skills and innovation.

Sustaining and refreshing your professional footprint requires ongoing attention. Create a quarterly review schedule to assess and refresh your online presence, and follow the steps mentioned earlier, from start to finish. Set calendar reminders to update your profiles after major accomplishments, new skills acquisition or role changes.

Follow relevant companies and thought leaders in your industry, to stay current on terminology and trends. Set Google alerts for key industry terms, to identify emerging concepts you should incorporate into your profiles.

Regularly contribute fresh content that demonstrates your evolving expertise. Even brief LinkedIn posts or comments on industry articles help maintain an active and up-to-date online reputation.

Request new recommendations after successful projects or collaborations. These provide fresh social proof and often contain current industry terminology.

Finally, periodically review your privacy settings across platforms, to ensure you're sharing professionally relevant information while protecting personal data. Remember that an AI-proof digital presence balances visibility with appropriate boundaries.

By strategically shaping your online visibility, with both automated systems and human evaluators in mind, you position yourself to highlight your capabilities in the evolving era of AI-driven hiring. The goal isn't to trick the algorithms, but to ensure they accurately recognize and value your true professional capabilities.

Skills of the Future Workforce: The Three Interconnected Pillars

While technical expertise remains critical, the criteria by which talent is evaluated are shifting. Recruiters, hiring managers and AI systems now prioritize a fusion of capabilities that extend beyond job-specific knowledge. To stay competitive, professionals must move beyond conventional credentials, and develop future-forward skills that reflect adaptability, strategic thinking and emotional intelligence.

AI thrives in domains requiring data processing, pattern recognition and machine-based decision-making. As these capabilities expand, human workers must reposition themselves where machines fall short, such as ethical reasoning, creativity, layered communication and collaborative problem-solving. The future belongs to those who can work alongside technology, while providing the human lens that machines fundamentally lack.

Rather than accumulating disconnected qualifications, the modern professional must pursue a balanced skill portfolio, one that aligns with evolving industry needs and anticipates future demands. These future-ready skills fall into three interconnected categories: *technical adaptability*, *human-centric capabilities* and *hybrid competencies*. Each category reinforces the others and represents a vital component of a sustainable and resilient career path.

1. *Technical Adaptability*

The ability to work with, interpret and adapt to new technologies is no longer optional, it's foundational. Technical adaptability is not merely about learning a programming language or mastering a tool; it's a mindset of ongoing learning and integration.

Computational thinking – the ability to break complex

challenges into structured, solvable parts – is central to this adaptability. It enables professionals to understand how machines process problems and where human intervention still adds irreplaceable value.

Data literacy is now required across all industries. Interpreting trends, asking critical questions and translating data insights into business action are essential skills. While AI can surface the data, it takes a human mind to provide context and judgment.

Learning agility rounds out this pillar. Rapidly acquiring new skills, tools or platforms ensures professionals stay relevant in fast-changing environments. Those who develop their own methods to assess emerging technologies – deciding what to learn now and what to monitor for later – will remain ahead of the curve.

Practical steps to build technical adaptability include exploring public datasets, practicing visualization tools and maintaining a technology radar, to track and trial emerging trends.

2. *Human-centric Capabilities*

In present times, where algorithms handle repetitive and

routine tasks, the uniquely human traits rise in value. These are the attributes that cannot be programmed or machine-replicated, and they play a vital role in leadership, team dynamics and innovation.

Emotional intelligence, including empathy, self-awareness and interpersonal sensitivity, strengthens workplace relationships and fosters inclusive cultures. It enables professionals to understand not just what is being said, but how and why.

Creative problem-solving is another high-impact trait. While AI can optimize known solutions, it cannot imagine what does not yet exist. Divergent and convergent thinking – generating possibilities and then refining them – become key differentiators.

Ethical judgment becomes more significant as AI systems begin to influence real-world decisions. Professionals must be prepared to assess the ethical implications of automation, data usage and machine-driven decision-making, advocating for fairness and responsible design.

To sharpen these skills, professionals can analyze ethical case studies, engage in design challenges with artificial constraints, and simulate real-world interpersonal scenarios, to improve emotional calibration and response.

3. *Hybrid Competencies*

The intersection of human and technical skill sets creates hybrid professionals: those who serve as translators, connectors and integrators across domains. These individuals are invaluable in AI-driven organizations.

Communication across technical boundaries involves making complex topics accessible to a broader audience. It bridges the divide between technical teams and business stakeholders, ensuring alignment and shared understanding.

Human-AI collaboration entails understanding how to complement algorithms with human insight. This includes knowing when to trust machine outputs and when to intervene, as well as offering input to improve how intelligent systems respond and evolve.

Adaptive decision-making blends data, context, ethics and stakeholder input. It is the skill of making informed, responsible choices even when information is incomplete, conflicting or rapidly evolving.

Professionals can build hybrid competencies through interdisciplinary learning, paired human-AI analysis exercises, and deliberate practice in simplifying technical material without losing accuracy.

Building a Personalized Skill-Development Plan

While the self-audit that we discussed earlier lays the foundation, by revealing how you're currently perceived across digital platforms and identifying gaps in your positioning and visibility, these next steps are about crafting a forward-looking strategy to fill skill gaps and evolve with industry demands. Developing future skills requires more than good intentions; it demands a deliberate strategy:

Start with an honest skills audit. Use structured tools to assess your current proficiency across technical, human-centric and hybrid categories. Ask peers or mentors to validate your assessment for objectivity.

Identify gaps. Compare your current capabilities with those demanded by your target industry or role. This step allows you to focus your efforts on high-impact areas.

Create a prioritized roadmap. Focus first on essential gaps that align with your career goals and emerging market trends. Balance this with skills that naturally align with your strengths and interests.

Set measurable learning outcomes. Replace vague goals like "Learn data analysis" with specific milestones, such as "*Complete a predictive modeling project using Python, with real-world data.*"

Choose blended learning methods. Mix online courses, hands-on projects, mentoring and reading. Apply what you learn in real or simulated environments, to reinforce understanding and build confidence.

Document your progress, build a visible portfolio of applied work and reflect on what you learn along the way, to enhance retention and deepen mastery.

Demonstrating Future-Ready Skills

Possessing the right skills is one thing; communicating them effectively is another. AI screening systems prioritize digital proof of performance.

Showcase skill projects in your portfolio, complete with outcomes and tools used.

Build narrative case studies that walk the viewer

through a challenge, your approach, the skills applied and the results achieved.

Earn and share micro-credentials or verifiable digital badges, that prove your capabilities to both algorithms and humans.

Finally, don't underestimate soft documentation, journaling reflections, receiving structured feedback from peers and continuously iterating on your learning process.

Personal Branding Strategy

This subchapter elevates the concept of personal branding from mere profile polishing to a layered, strategic framework, which speaks fluently to both intelligent algorithms and human decision-makers. It explores how to build a reputation that adapts, amplifies and advances, in an era defined by adaptive algorithms.

Personal branding has evolved from a static résumé or a confident handshake into a dynamic, algorithm-conscious identity. Much of what defines an effective personal brand in today's AI-driven world has already been covered throughout this book, from keyword-optimized profiles and data-backed storytelling to content strategy and cross-platform consistency. These core practices form the foundation of an optimized, future-ready presence.

However, as AI systems become more sophisticated, strategic personal branding must now account for emerging dimensions that go far beyond surface-level polish. Modern algorithms are not only parsing the *what* of your message but also the *how*, the tone and the emotional signals embedded in your communication.

Sentiment analysis, for example, allows AI systems to interpret the emotional tone of your language. Whether you're writing a LinkedIn post or responding to a public comment, algorithms can detect positivity, empathy, assertiveness or even defensiveness, assessing how well your communication style fits the cultural expectations of a particular role or organization. Maintaining a tone that is both emotionally perceptive and professionally engaging has never been more important.

Equally valuable is the integration of interactive elements into your professional online identity. From clickable portfolios and dynamic dashboards to short video introductions or embedded client feedback, these features increase engagement while feeding intelligent hiring tools richer behavioral data. Interaction metrics – such as dwell time, engagement flow and click-through depth – help platforms assess the authenticity and appeal of your professional profile.

Another evolving consideration is attribution clarity. In team-based environments, AI tools may struggle to understand individual contribution unless you explicitly articulate it. When discussing collaborative projects, specify your unique role, decisions you made, tools you employed, and the measurable impact that you personally generated within the team. Clarity here not only aids recruiters, it ensures AI systems correctly attribute expertise and effectiveness.

In short, strategic personal branding in the AI era is no longer about self-promotion; it's about structured visibility, measurable authenticity and intelligent positioning. As algorithms continue to shape first impressions, your ability to align both your message and your methods with these new systems will determine whether your brand rises above the noise, or gets filtered out before a human ever sees it.

Five Transition Success Stories

The job-market transformation hit Rachel Cox like a brick wall. After ten years as a marketing manager at a retail company, she found herself suddenly unemployed when her department was restructured. Armed with a polished résumé that had secured her previous positions, Rachel confidently applied to dozens of marketing roles – only to face silence. "I kept wondering why I wasn't even getting interviews," she recalls. "My résumé highlighted my experience, managing campaigns that increased sales by twenty percent, and my MBA from a respected university. In the past, that was enough."

Rachel's experience reflects the jarring reality many professionals face, when they discover that traditional job-seeking methods no longer work in today's algorithm-led hiring environment. Her wake-up call came during a networking event, where a recruiter mentioned that her application likely never made it past the company's AI screening tools. "He explained that my résumé lacked the specific keywords their system was programmed to identify, so, despite my qualifications, I was automatically filtered out."

This revelation prompted Rachel to completely reimagine her approach. She began by researching the AI tools companies in her industry were using, and understanding how they evaluated candidates. She used LinkedIn's "Skills Assessment" feature, to identify and verify her marketable skills, then restructured her online profiles to highlight these capabilities with industry-specific terminology. She created a personal website, showcasing case studies of her marketing campaigns, complete with visual data representations of her results and video explanations of her strategies.

"The difference was immediate," Rachel says. "Within two weeks of optimizing my digital presence, I received interview requests from three companies that had previously ignored my applications." Six weeks later, she accepted a position as a digital marketing director at a tech startup – at a salary 15% higher than her previous role.

Rachel's transition success hinged on several key strategies: understanding how AI screening tools work, adapting her presentation to be machine-readable while remaining authentic, and creating a multi-platform presence that demonstrated her skills rather than just claiming them.

Taimour Baig's story offers another perspective on navigating the new terrain. As a self-taught software developer without a Computer Science degree, Taimour struggled to get past the first round of applications, despite having built several successful mobile apps. "Companies were using degree requirements as a proxy for skills," he explains. "Their automated hiring tools were programmed to prioritize candidates with formal education credentials."

Rather than continuing to fight this uphill battle, Taimour leveraged the shift toward skills-based hiring, by creating a comprehensive GitHub portfolio and participating in coding challenges on widely used competitive programming platforms. He earned badges and certifications through IBM's developer program and Google's certification courses, building a verifiable skill profile that AI systems could easily recognize.

"I stopped trying to fit my experience into a traditional résumé format," Taimour says. "Instead, I crafted an online profile that directly reflected the demonstrable coding skills and problem-solving abilities those companies were searching for."

Taimour also used a global data science competition platform, known for real-world machine-learning challenges, to showcase his machine-learning expertise, placing in the top 10% in two challenges. He created video walkthroughs of his coding process and published them on YouTube, generating over fifty thousand views and establishing his authority in specific programming languages.

His breakthrough came when a tech company's AI talent discovery system identified him, based on his GitHub contributions and competition rankings. "They reached out to me directly; I never even applied. The hiring manager told me their system flagged me as a high-potential candidate based on my demonstrated skills, not my résumé." Taimour now works as a senior developer at a financial technology company, earning more than many of his peers with advanced degrees.

The key lessons from Taimour's experience include focusing on verifiable skill demonstrations rather than credentials, creating content that showcases problem-solving processes, and participating in platforms where AI recruitment systems actively search for talent.

For Mahnoor Ali, a mid-career finance professional, the challenge was different. With fifteen years of experience in traditional banking, she wanted to transition to financial technology but found her applications consistently rejected. "My résumé screamed 'traditional banker' to the machine-led hiring filters," she explains. "I needed to reframe my experience, to show its relevance to fintech."

Mahnoor's transformation began with a skills-gap analysis. She used LinkedIn's job postings to identify the specific technical skills fintech companies were seeking, then compared them with her existing capabilities. She discovered that, while she had strong financial knowledge, she lacked the data-analysis and technology-integration skills these companies prioritized.

Rather than immediately applying for jobs, Mahnoor invested six months in targeted skill development. She completed a Data Science bootcamp, earned certifications in SQL and Python, and participated in open-banking hackathons. Crucially, she documented this learning journey publicly, creating weekly LinkedIn posts about her progress and insights.

"I treated my transition as a project and made my

learning process visible," Mahnoor says. "This accomplished two things: it demonstrated my commitment to acquiring relevant skills and it created a digital trail that AI systems could detect."

Mahnoor also leveraged asynchronous video interviews to her advantage. When invited to complete video assessments, she practiced extensively, focusing on using industry-specific terminology that AI analysis tools would recognize, while maintaining a natural speaking style. She researched each company's values and strategically incorporated them into her responses.

After her six-month skill-development period, Mahnoor secured a position as a product manager at a fintech startup. "The hiring manager told me they were impressed by my commitment to learning new skills, and my ability to bridge traditional finance and technology," she says. "My video interviews scored highly in their AI analysis, for both technical knowledge and cultural fit."

Mahnoor's success highlights the importance of identifying and addressing skill gaps, documenting your learning journey publicly, and preparing specifically for AI-analyzed video interviews.

Adam Baker's transition story demonstrates how strategic personal branding can counter biases embedded in machine-led screening systems. As a 52-year-old marketing executive, Adam found himself struggling against algorithm-driven filters that seemed to favor younger candidates with digital-native skills.

"I realized that the algorithms were picking up on subtle signals in my résumé that dated me," Adam explains. "References to older technologies and techniques were likely causing the AI to categorize me as less current, regardless of my actual capabilities."

Adam worked with a digital-identity consultant to reshape his online presence. They removed graduation dates from his profiles, updated his professional headshots, and carefully audited his language for dated terminology. More importantly, they created a content strategy that positioned Adam as an authority on integrating traditional marketing wisdom with emerging technologies.

He began publishing articles on Medium about applying time-tested marketing principles to digital channels, created infographics comparing marketing metrics across generations, and launched a podcast interviewing both veteran marketers and digital newcomers. This content strategy generated substantial engagement, with his articles being shared by industry influencers.

"I stopped trying to hide my experience, and instead reframed it as a unique advantage," Adam says. "By creating content that demonstrated my understanding of both traditional and digital approaches, I changed how the algorithms categorized me."

Adam also leveraged AI tools proactively, using services like Jobscan to optimize his application materials for specific job postings, and Crystal to analyze the communication preferences of potential employers. He used these insights to tailor his outreach messages and interview responses.

Within four months, Adam secured a Chief Marketing Officer position at a growing e-commerce company. "The CEO later told me that my content had initially caught their attention, and my strategic approach to the interview process confirmed I was the right fit," he says.

Adam's experience underscores the importance of proactively managing how AI systems categorize you, creating content that demonstrates current knowledge, and using AI tools strategically in your job search.

For recent graduate Marjan Rabiei, the challenge was standing out in a sea of candidates with similar educational backgrounds. "I was applying for Entry-Level Data Analyst positions, along with thousands of other new graduates with similar degrees," she explains. "I needed to find a way to differentiate myself, in a process largely controlled by AI."

Marjan's strategy focused on creating quantifiable evidence of her capabilities through practical projects. She participated in online data challenges, created visualizations on Tableau Public and contributed to open-source data projects. For each project, she wrote detailed methodology explanations and created video walkthroughs explaining her analytical process.

She also leveraged gamified assessment platforms like Pymetrics and HackerRank, completing their public challenges and sharing her results. "These platforms gave me objective, third-party verification of my skills that AI screening tools could easily process," Marjan says.

Perhaps most innovatively, Marjan created data-analysis projects specifically tailored to each company she applied to. "Before applying to a retail company, I analyzed their publicly available data, and created visualizations showing potential optimization opportunities," she explains. "I included these in my application, as examples of the value I could bring."

This approach led to multiple interview offers, and Marjan ultimately accepted a position at a healthcare analytics firm. "The hiring manager mentioned that my custom analysis project caught their attention, because it demonstrated both technical skills and initiative," she says.

Marjan's success highlights the effectiveness of creating company-specific work samples, leveraging third-party skill-verification platforms, and documenting your analytical process publicly.

These success stories are not outliers. They are signals of a new era, where those who understand the evolving rules of visibility, adaptability and self-presentation will define the future of work. The résumé may be dying, but your digital presence is just beginning to speak on your behalf. Make sure it speaks with clarity, credibility and courage.

The future of work isn't waiting; it's already rewriting the rules. From algorithms that screen candidates to platforms that reward visibility over pedigree, the game has changed. But with change comes opportunity. Those who choose to adapt, experiment and evolve will find not only new doors opening, but new ways to define success on their own terms.

Don't shy away from the future. Shape it.

About the Author

Nadeem Lutfullah is a global recruitment and training expert, freelance HR consultant and career mentor, with four decades of corporate experience in the aviation HR industry. He has helped thousands of individuals navigate their career journeys, many rising to positions beyond their initial aspirations.

Known for his strategic guidance and deeply human approach, Nadeem is passionate about helping others thrive in an era of data-driven hiring. His workshops, books and career interventions continue to inspire professionals to redefine success on their own terms.

This book is a continuation of his enduring desire not only to share the insights drawn from his rich professional past, but also to equip today's workforce – and those of tomorrow – with the clarity and resilience needed to adapt to the challenges we already see unfolding. His work serves as both a reflection and a roadmap for anyone striving to remain relevant, resourceful and ready, in a rapidly changing world.

Also by Nadeem Lutfullah

Find the Ladder

A groundbreaking guide for job-seekers and career professionals navigating the post-pandemic job market. Published June 2024.

📖 Available on Amazon:

https://www.amazon.com/dp/B0D6PCYMR7

55 Unconventional Interview Questions

A fresh, thought-provoking approach to mastering interviews in the age of AI, behavioral assessments and non-traditional hiring.

Published November 2024.

📖 Available on Amazon:

https://www.amazon.com/dp/9695492142

I'd value your feedback.

If this book offered you clarity, guidance or a fresh perspective, I'd be truly grateful if you took a moment to leave an honest review.

Your insights not only help others discover the value within these pages; they also encourage me to keep writing and sharing.

Thank you for being part of the journey.

www.ingramcontent.com/pod-product-compliance
Lightning Source LLC
LaVergne TN
LVHW021225080526
838199LV00089B/5831